# GRASSHOPPERS

## VALERIE BODDEN

Published by Creative Education

P.O. Box 227, Mankato, Minnesota 56002

Creative Education is an imprint of The Creative Company

Design and production by Stephanie Blumenthal

Printed in the United States of America

Photographs by John Capinera, Whitney Cranshaw, Entomological Society of America / Ries Memorial Slide Collection, Howard Ensign Evans, Getty Images (Charles Krebs, National Geographic, SEA STUDIOS, Tamara Staples, Louise Tanguay), Photo Disk

Library of Congress Cataloging-in-Publication Data

Bodden, Valerie.

Grasshoppers / by Valerie Bodden.

p. cm. — (BugBooks)

Includes index.

ISBN-13: 978-1-58341-544-3

1. Grasshoppers—Juvenile literature. I. Title. II. Series.

QL508.A2B57 2007

595.7'26—DC22     2006017037

First Edition

2 4 6 8 9 7 5 3 1

A LOUD BUZZ FILLS THE AIR. ALL OF A SUDDEN, YOU SEE LOTS AND LOTS OF GRASSHOPPERS. THEY ARE FLYING THROUGH THE SKY. THE GRASSHOPPERS LAND ON FIELDS. THEY EAT THE PLANTS IN THE FIELDS. WHEN THEY ARE DONE, ALL OF THE PLANTS ARE GONE!

GRASSHOPPERS ARE INSECTS. MOST GRASSHOPPERS ARE GREEN.

 BUT SOME ARE BROWN. OTHER GRASSHOPPERS ARE BLACK. MOST GRASSHOPPERS ARE SMALL. BUT ONE KIND OF GRASSHOPPER IS VERY BIG. SOME-TIMES PEOPLE THINK IT IS A BIRD!

*There are many kinds of grasshoppers.*

GRASSHOPPERS HAVE BIG EYES.
THEY CAN SEE VERY WELL. THEY
HAVE A BIG
MOUTH, TOO.
GRASSHOPPERS
DO NOT HAVE A NOSE. THEY USE
THEIR ANTENNAE (AN-*TEN*-NAY)
TO SMELL THINGS. THEIR ANTEN-
NAE HELP THEM FEEL THINGS, TOO.

*Grasshoppers' eyes stick out from their heads.*

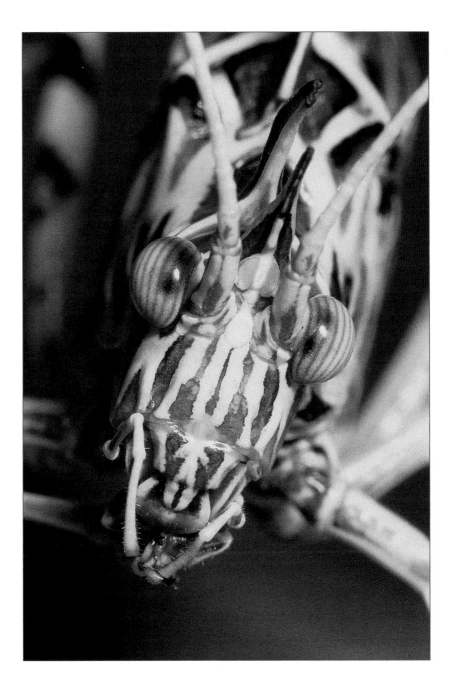

BLENDING IN  *Green grasshoppers blend in with grass. Brown grasshoppers blend in with dirt. Blending in helps grasshoppers hide from animals that want to eat them.*

GRASSHOPPERS HAVE SIX LEGS.

THEIR LEGS ARE VERY STRONG.

 GRASSHOPPERS' BACK

LEGS ARE LONG. THEY

STICK UP ABOVE THE

GRASSHOPPER'S BODY. GRASSHOP-

PERS USE THEIR LEGS TO JUMP.

GRASSHOPPERS CAN JUMP VERY HIGH!

*Grasshoppers can be hard to see on leaves and grass.*

MOST GRASSHOPPERS HAVE WINGS.

SOME GRASSHOPPERS CAN FLY FAST.

OTHERS CAN FLY FAR. SOME GRASS-

HOPPERS CANNOT FLY. THEY USE

THEIR WINGS TO GLIDE.

*Grasshoppers tuck their wings against their bodies.*

BABY GRASSHOPPERS HATCH
FROM EGGS. THEY ARE CALLED
"NYMPHS" (*NIMFS*). NYMPHS LOOK
LIKE GROWN-UP GRASSHOPPERS.
BUT NYMPHS DO NOT HAVE WINGS.

*Nymphs lose their old skin when they become adults.*

  13

GRASSHOPPERS LIVE ALL OVER
THE WORLD. THEY LIKE WARM PLACES.
YOU CAN FIND GRASSHOPPERS IN
FIELDS. YOU CAN FIND THEM IN THE
GRASS. SOME GRASSHOPPERS LIVE IN
TREES. OTHERS LIVE IN DESERTS.

*Some grasshoppers rest in sand. Others rest on flowers.*

WARMING UP  Most grasshoppers need to be warm to move. If they are too cold, they sit in the sun to warm up.

GRASSHOPPERS EAT A LOT. THEY

 LOVE TO EAT PLANTS!

SOME GRASSHOPPERS

EAT GRASS. OTHERS

EAT FLOWERS. SOME GRASSHOPPERS

EAT PLANTS GROWING IN FIELDS.

*Grasshoppers can hurt plants if they eat too much.*

Lots of animals like to eat grasshoppers. Birds like to eat grasshoppers. So do frogs and skunks. Mice eat grasshoppers, too. Even cats like to eat grasshoppers!

*Grasshoppers try to hide from frogs and other animals.*

A Tasty Snack   Some people eat grasshoppers. Grasshoppers can be cooked in lots of ways. Some people like lollipops with grasshoppers in the middle!

LOTS OF GRASSHOPPERS  *There are lots of different kinds of grasshoppers. The cricket is one kind of grasshopper. The locust (LOH-KUST) is a kind of grasshopper, too. So is the katydid (KAY-TEE-DID).*

MOST GRASSHOPPERS CHIRP. EACH KIND OF GRASSHOPPER MAKES ITS OWN KIND OF CHIRP. GRASSHOPPERS' CHIRPS SOUND VERY PRETTY. IN THE SUMMER, YOU CAN HEAR THEIR CHIRPS FILL THE AIR!

*Like most grasshoppers, pink katydids can chirp.*

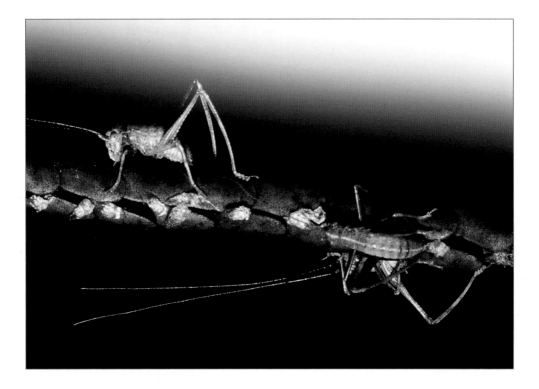

ANTENNAE — THE TWO LONG RODS ON TOP OF A

GRASSHOPPER'S HEAD

DESERTS — HOT, DRY AREAS WITH LOTS OF SAND AND FEW PLANTS

GLIDE — FLOAT THROUGH THE AIR WITHOUT FLAPPING WINGS

INSECTS — BUGS THAT HAVE SIX LEGS

# INDEX

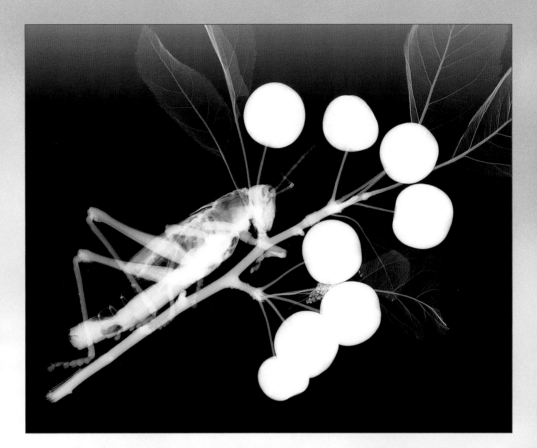